Because I love You

Gift Certificate

By

Samuel Singleton

© 2002 by Samuel Singleton. All rights reserved.

No part of this book may be reproduced, stored in a retrieval system, or transmitted by any means, electronic, mechanical, photocopying, recording, or otherwise, without written permission from the author.

ISBN: 1-4033-3757-8 (e-book)
ISBN: 1-4033-3758-6 (Paperback)

This book is printed on acid free paper.

INTRODUCTION

Most men and women feel that their primary goal in life is to find that one special person. They will go to any length to achieve this goal. After reaching it, they become lax, content in the knowledge that the person they were pursuing is now their mate forever.

You and I know this is not true. We realize that in order for us to remain together, to grow together, that we must continue to work on our relationship. We are aware that should we stop working, our relationship will dry up as fast as a rose planted in the desert.

You and I will make this Gift Certificate our friend. We'll use it to make sure our love for each other will grow stronger, longer.

Because
I Love You
CERTIFICATE

Presented to:

In honor of the special relationship we have developed. This is a relationship unlike any other in the Universe. This Gift Certificate and the contents herein is to be used to ensure that the love we have for each other will continue to grow throughout our lives.

_____
(Signature)

CONTENTS

1. A Walk on the Beach at Night 1
2. A Trip 9
3. A Massage 17
4. Dinner 25
5. Shopping 33
6. Broadway Play 41
7. Dancing 49
8. A Trip to Nowhere 57
9. A Relaxing day at the Zoo 65
10. Camping 73
11. Sailing 81
12. Go Kart Racing 89
13. Church 97
14. Jamaica 105
15. A Stroll 113
16. Expensive Meal 121

Because I Love You Gift Certificate

A Walk on the Beach at Night

The ocean brings with it a certain serenity that is hard to find anywhere else on earth. The waves crashing against the rocks as the tide comes in will seem to beg you to let go, to reach out and embrace life.

Ask me to join you. Let us take a stroll along the beach at night. We will gaze together at the red sun as it drops behind the horizon. Our feet will dig into the soft wet sand as we walk, holding hand and enjoying each other.

"You bet! I want to take this walk on _____"
　　　　　　　　　　　　　　　　　　　　(Date)

　　　　　　　　_____
　　　　　　　　　(My signature)

Samuel Singleton

A Walk on the Beach at Night

The ocean brings with it a certain serenity that is hard to find anywhere else on earth. The waves crashing against the rocks as the tide comes in will seem to beg you to let go, to reach out and embrace life.

Ask me to join you. Let us take a stroll along the beach at night. We will gaze together at the red sun as it drops behind the horizon. Our feet will dig into the soft wet sand as we walk, holding hand and enjoying each other.

"You bet! I want to take this walk on _____"
                                                    (Date)

_____
(My signature)

Because I Love You Gift Certificate

A Walk on the Beach at Night

The ocean brings with it a certain serenity that is hard to find anywhere else on earth. The waves crashing against the rocks as the tide comes in will seem to beg you to let go, to reach out and embrace life.

Ask me to join you. Let us take a stroll along the beach at night. We will gaze together at the red sun as it drops behind the horizon. Our feet will dig into the soft wet sand as we walk, holding hand and enjoying each other.

"You bet! I want to take this walk on _____"
(Date)

_____
(My signature)

Samuel Singleton

A Walk on the Beach at Night

The ocean brings with it a certain serenity that is hard to find anywhere else on earth. The waves crashing against the rocks as the tide comes in will seem to beg you to let go, to reach out and embrace life.

Ask me to join you. Let us take a stroll along the beach at night. We will gaze together at the red sun as it drops behind the horizon. Our feet will dig into the soft wet sand as we walk, holding hand and enjoying each other.

"You bet! I want to take this walk on _____"
                                    (Date)

_____
(My signature)

Because I Love You Gift Certificate

A Walk on the Beach at Night

The ocean brings with it a certain serenity that is hard to find anywhere else on earth. The waves crashing against the rocks as the tide comes in will seem to beg you to let go, to reach out and embrace life.

Ask me to join you. Let us take a stroll along the beach at night. We will gaze together at the red sun as it drops behind the horizon. Our feet will dig into the soft wet sand as we walk, holding hand and enjoying each other.

"You bet! I want to take this walk on _____"
(Date)

_____
(My signature)

Samuel Singleton

A Walk on the Beach at Night

The ocean brings with it a certain serenity that is hard to find anywhere else on earth. The waves crashing against the rocks as the tide comes in will seem to beg you to let go, to reach out and embrace life.

Ask me to join you. Let us take a stroll along the beach at night. We will gaze together at the red sun as it drops behind the horizon. Our feet will dig into the soft wet sand as we walk, holding hand and enjoying each other.

"You bet! I want to take this walk on _____"
                                            (Date)

_____
(My signature)

Because I Love You Gift Certificate

A Walk on the Beach at Night

The ocean brings with it a certain serenity that is hard to find anywhere else on earth. The waves crashing against the rocks as the tide comes in will seem to beg you to let go, to reach out and embrace life.

Ask me to join you. Let us take a stroll along the beach at night. We will gaze together at the red sun as it drops behind the horizon. Our feet will dig into the soft wet sand as we walk, holding hand and enjoying each other.

"You bet! I want to take this walk on _____"
(Date)

_____
(My signature)

Samuel Singleton

Because I Love You Gift Certificate

A Trip

It's been a long, demanding week at work. The boss never calmed down and the workers seemed ready to walk out en masse. Now Friday has come. The time to leave the boss, workers, and the problems behind.

Let's get in the car or on an airplane and take off. What will be our destination? As long as we are together where we end up will not matter.

"We're 'outta' here on _____"
                              (Date)

_____
(My Signature)

Samuel Singleton

A Trip

It's been a long, demanding week at work. The boss never calmed down and the workers seemed ready to walk out en masse. Now Friday has come. The time to leave the boss, workers, and the problems behind.

Let's get in the car or on an airplane and take off. What will be our destination? As long as we are together where we end up will not matter.

"We're 'outta' here on _____"
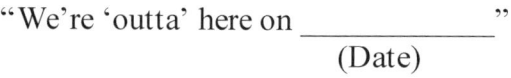
(Date)

_____
(My Signature)

Because I Love You Gift Certificate

A Trip

It's been a long, demanding week at work. The boss never calmed down and the workers seemed ready to walk out en masse. Now Friday has come. The time to leave the boss, workers, and the problems behind.

Let's get in the car or on an airplane and take off. What will be our destination? As long as we are together where we end up will not matter.

"We're 'outta' here on _____"
                            (Date)

_____
(My Signature)

Samuel Singleton

A Trip

It's been a long, demanding week at work. The boss never calmed down and the workers seemed ready to walk out en masse. Now Friday has come. The time to leave the boss, workers, and the problems behind.

Let's get in the car or on an airplane and take off. What will be our destination? As long as we are together where we end up will not matter.

"We're 'outta' here on _____"
                              (Date)

_____
(My Signature)

Because I Love You Gift Certificate

A Trip

It's been a long, demanding week at work. The boss never calmed down and the workers seemed ready to walk out en masse. Now Friday has come. The time to leave the boss, workers, and the problems behind.

Let's get in the car or on an airplane and take off. What will be our destination? As long as we are together where we end up will not matter.

"We're 'outta' here on _____"
(Date)

_____
(My Signature)

Samuel Singleton

A Trip

It's been a long, demanding week at work. The boss never calmed down and the workers seemed ready to walk out en masse. Now Friday has come. The time to leave the boss, workers, and the problems behind.

Let's get in the car or on an airplane and take off. What will be our destination? As long as we are together where we end up will not matter.

"We're 'outta' here on _____"
                              (Date)

_____
(My Signature)

Because I Love You Gift Certificate

A Trip

It's been a long, demanding week at work. The boss never calmed down and the workers seemed ready to walk out en masse. Now Friday has come. The time to leave the boss, workers, and the problems behind.

Let's get in the car or on an airplane and take off. What will be our destination? As long as we are together where we end up will not matter.

"We're 'outta' here on _____"
                          (Date)

_____
(My Signature)

Samuel Singleton

Because I Love You Gift Certificate

A Massage

I love how hands so strong and hard can touch with the gentleness of a butterfly landing on a rose petal. I love the way the start at the neck and work their way down the entire body, taking the body into another dimension as they travel. Those hands belong to you.

"That body belongs to me! Let's bring them together on _____."
(Date)

_____
(My Signature)

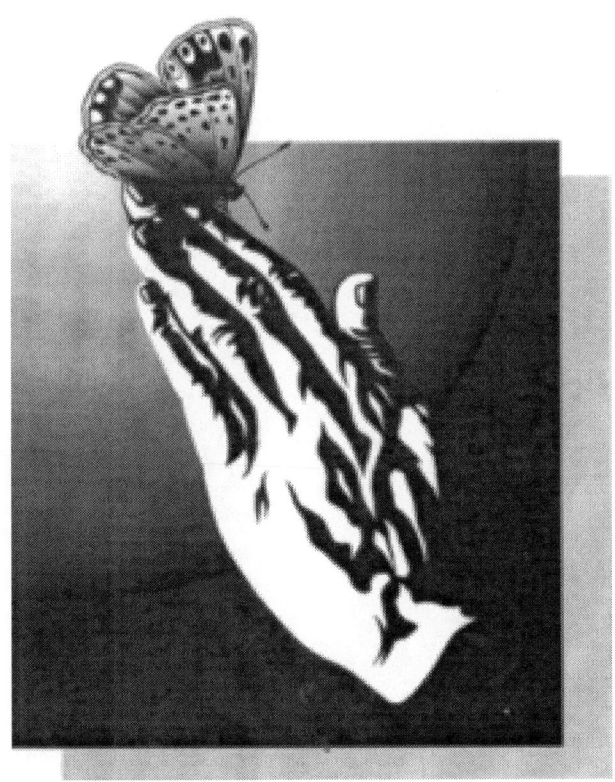

Samuel Singleton

A Massage

I love how hands so strong and hard can touch with the gentleness of a butterfly landing on a rose petal. I love the way the start at the neck and work their way down the entire body, taking the body into another dimension as they travel. Those hands belong to you.

"That body belongs to me! Let's bring them together on ."

(Date)

(My Signature)

Because I Love You Gift Certificate

A Massage

I love how hands so strong and hard can touch with the gentleness of a butterfly landing on a rose petal. I love the way the start at the neck and work their way down the entire body, taking the body into another dimension as they travel. Those hands belong to you.

"That body belongs to me! Let's bring them together on _____."
(Date)

_____
(My Signature)

Samuel Singleton

A Massage

I love how hands so strong and hard can touch with the gentleness of a butterfly landing on a rose petal. I love the way the start at the neck and work their way down the entire body, taking the body into another dimension as they travel. Those hands belong to you.

"That body belongs to me! Let's bring them together on _____."

(Date)

(My Signature)

Because I Love You Gift Certificate

A Massage

I love how hands so strong and hard can touch with the gentleness of a butterfly landing on a rose petal. I love the way the start at the neck and work their way down the entire body, taking the body into another dimension as they travel. Those hands belong to you.

"That body belongs to me! Let's bring them together on _____."
(Date)

_____
(My Signature)

Samuel Singleton

A Massage

    I love how hands so strong and hard can touch with the gentleness of a butterfly landing on a rose petal. I love the way the start at the neck and work their way down the entire body, taking the body into another dimension as they travel. Those hands belong to you.

    "That body belongs to me! Let's bring them together on ."
(Date)

_____
(My Signature)

Because I Love You Gift Certificate

A Massage

I love how hands so strong and hard can touch with the gentleness of a butterfly landing on a rose petal. I love the way the start at the neck and work their way down the entire body, taking the body into another dimension as they travel. Those hands belong to you.

"That body belongs to me! Let's bring them together on _____."
(Date)

_____
(My Signature)

Samuel Singleton

Because I Love You Gift Certificate

Dinner

Couples always talk of their favorite Restaurant. It's the eatery where the ambience seems to enhance an already perfect evening. It's the eatery where we are among so many people yet are still alone.

You and I will get among the crowd of eaters so that we can spend some time alone.

"I will be oh so hungry on _____"
            (Date)

_____
(My Signature)

Samuel Singleton

Dinner

Couples always talk of their favorite Restaurant. It's the eatery where the ambience seems to enhance an already perfect evening. It's the eatery where we are among so many people yet are still alone.

You and I will get among the crowd of eaters so that we can spend some time alone.

"I will be oh so hungry on _____"
                              (Date)

_____
(My Signature)

Because I Love You Gift Certificate

Dinner

Couples always talk of their favorite Restaurant. It's the eatery where the ambience seems to enhance an already perfect evening. It's the eatery where we are among so many people yet are still alone.

You and I will get among the crowd of eaters so that we can spend some time alone.

"I will be oh so hungry on _____"
                              (Date)

_____
(My Signature)

Samuel Singleton

Dinner

    Couples always talk of their favorite Restaurant. It's the eatery where the ambience seems to enhance an already perfect evening. It's the eatery where we are among so many people yet are still alone.

    You and I will get among the crowd of eaters so that we can spend some time alone.

"I will be oh so hungry on _____"
                                (Date)

_____
(My Signature)

Because I Love You Gift Certificate

Dinner

Couples always talk of their favorite Restaurant. It's the eatery where the ambience seems to enhance an already perfect evening. It's the eatery where we are among so many people yet are still alone.

You and I will get among the crowd of eaters so that we can spend some time alone.

"I will be oh so hungry on _____"
(Date)

_____
(My Signature)

Samuel Singleton

Dinner

Couples always talk of their favorite Restaurant. It's the eatery where the ambience seems to enhance an already perfect evening. It's the eatery where we are among so many people yet are still alone.

You and I will get among the crowd of eaters so that we can spend some time alone.

"I will be oh so hungry on _____"
                                                (Date)

_____
(My Signature)

Because I Love You Gift Certificate

Dinner

Couples always talk of their favorite Restaurant. It's the eatery where the ambience seems to enhance an already perfect evening. It's the eatery where we are among so many people yet are still alone.

You and I will get among the crowd of eaters so that we can spend some time alone.

"I will be oh so hungry on _____"
      (Date)

_____
(My Signature)

Samuel Singleton

Because I Love You Gift Certificate

Shopping

It's been said that men hate to go shopping with women because that look at and try on everything in the store. Women will say that they would want men with them as they try on clothes but hate seeing the board looks they show.

You and I are different. We know that shopping gives us yet another reason to be together. We'll look around, go to different shops, and try on clothes. The we'll end the day at our favorite Sports Bar and Grill, eating a burger and swilling a beer.

"Hey! We can also catch that game. I need us to get together on _____."
(Date)

_____
(My Signature)

Shopping

It's been said that men hate to go shopping with women because that look at and try on everything in the store. Women will say that they would want men with them as they try on clothes but hate seeing the board looks they show.

You and I are different. We know that shopping gives us yet another reason to be together. We'll look around, go to different shops, and try on clothes. The we'll end the day at our favorite Sports Bar and Grill, eating a burger and swilling a beer.

"Hey! We can also catch that game. I need us to get together on _____."

(Date)

_____
(My Signature)

Because I Love You Gift Certificate

Shopping

It's been said that men hate to go shopping with women because that look at and try on everything in the store. Women will say that they would want men with them as they try on clothes but hate seeing the board looks they show.

You and I are different. We know that shopping gives us yet another reason to be together. We'll look around, go to different shops, and try on clothes. The we'll end the day at our favorite Sports Bar and Grill, eating a burger and swilling a beer.

"Hey! We can also catch that game. I need us to get together on _____."
(Date)

_____
(My Signature)

Samuel Singleton

Shopping

It's been said that men hate to go shopping with women because that look at and try on everything in the store. Women will say that they would want men with them as they try on clothes but hate seeing the board looks they show.

You and I are different. We know that shopping gives us yet another reason to be together. We'll look around, go to different shops, and try on clothes. The we'll end the day at our favorite Sports Bar and Grill, eating a burger and swilling a beer.

"Hey! We can also catch that game. I need us to get together on _____."

(Date)

_____
(My Signature)

Because I Love You Gift Certificate

Shopping

It's been said that men hate to go shopping with women because that look at and try on everything in the store. Women will say that they would want men with them as they try on clothes but hate seeing the board looks they show.

You and I are different. We know that shopping gives us yet another reason to be together. We'll look around, go to different shops, and try on clothes. The we'll end the day at our favorite Sports Bar and Grill, eating a burger and swilling a beer.

"Hey! We can also catch that game. I need us to get together on _____."
(Date)

_____
(My Signature)

Samuel Singleton

Shopping

It's been said that men hate to go shopping with women because that look at and try on everything in the store. Women will say that they would want men with them as they try on clothes but hate seeing the board looks they show.

You and I are different. We know that shopping gives us yet another reason to be together. We'll look around, go to different shops, and try on clothes. The we'll end the day at our favorite Sports Bar and Grill, eating a burger and swilling a beer.

"Hey! We can also catch that game. I need us to get together on _____ "

(Date)

_____
(My Signature)

Because I Love You Gift Certificate

Shopping

It's been said that men hate to go shopping with women because that look at and try on everything in the store. Women will say that they would want men with them as they try on clothes but hate seeing the board looks they show.

You and I are different. We know that shopping gives us yet another reason to be together. We'll look around, go to different shops, and try on clothes. The we'll end the day at our favorite Sports Bar and Grill, eating a burger and swilling a beer.

"Hey! We can also catch that game. I need us to get together on _____."
(Date)

_____
(My Signature)

Samuel Singleton

Because I Love You Gift Certificate

Broadway Play

New York! It's been called the theatrical district of the world. It's called that because if you want to see a Play, no matter how obscure it might be, you'll find it in New York.

We'll get a copy of the New Yorker, find a play that will make us laugh, then set a date. The Play is only a short flight and hotel room away. We will shop, sightsee, and sample some of the fine cuisine New York offers. A carriage ride through Central Park will highlight what will be a fantastic weekend.

"Just the trip to New York is in itself fantastic! We'll leave town on _____"
     (Date)

_____
(My Signature)

Samuel Singleton

Broadway Play

New York! It's been called the theatrical district of the world. It's called that because if you want to see a Play, no matter how obscure it might be, you'll find it in New York.

We'll get a copy of the New Yorker, find a play that will make us laugh, then set a date. The Play is only a short flight and hotel room away. We will shop, sightsee, and sample some of the fine cuisine New York offers. A carriage ride through Central Park will highlight what will be a fantastic weekend.

"Just the trip to New York is in itself fantastic! We'll leave town on _____"
    (Date)

_____
(My Signature)

Because I Love You Gift Certificate

Broadway Play

New York! It's been called the theatrical district of the world. It's called that because if you want to see a Play, no matter how obscure it might be, you'll find it in New York.

We'll get a copy of the New Yorker, find a play that will make us laugh, then set a date. The Play is only a short flight and hotel room away. We will shop, sightsee, and sample some of the fine cuisine New York offers. A carriage ride through Central Park will highlight what will be a fantastic weekend.

"Just the trip to New York is in itself fantastic! We'll leave town on _____"
      (Date)

_____
(My Signature)

Samuel Singleton

Broadway Play

New York! It's been called the theatrical district of the world. It's called that because if you want to see a Play, no matter how obscure it might be, you'll find it in New York.

We'll get a copy of the New Yorker, find a play that will make us laugh, then set a date. The Play is only a short flight and hotel room away. We will shop, sightsee, and sample some of the fine cuisine New York offers. A carriage ride through Central Park will highlight what will be a fantastic weekend.

"Just the trip to New York is in itself fantastic! We'll leave town on _____"
  (Date)

_____
(My Signature)

Because I Love You Gift Certificate

Broadway Play

New York! It's been called the theatrical district of the world. It's called that because if you want to see a Play, no matter how obscure it might be, you'll find it in New York.

We'll get a copy of the New Yorker, find a play that will make us laugh, then set a date. The Play is only a short flight and hotel room away. We will shop, sightsee, and sample some of the fine cuisine New York offers. A carriage ride through Central Park will highlight what will be a fantastic weekend.

"Just the trip to New York is in itself fantastic! We'll leave town on _____"
    (Date)

_____
(My Signature)

Samuel Singleton

Broadway Play

New York! It's been called the theatrical district of the world. It's called that because if you want to see a Play, no matter how obscure it might be, you'll find it in New York.

We'll get a copy of the New Yorker, find a play that will make us laugh, then set a date. The Play is only a short flight and hotel room away. We will shop, sightsee, and sample some of the fine cuisine New York offers. A carriage ride through Central Park will highlight what will be a fantastic weekend.

"Just the trip to New York is in itself fantastic! We'll leave town on _____"
    (Date)

_____
(My Signature)

Because I Love You Gift Certificate

Broadway Play

New York! It's been called the theatrical district of the world. It's called that because if you want to see a Play, no matter how obscure it might be, you'll find it in New York.

We'll get a copy of the New Yorker, find a play that will make us laugh, then set a date. The Play is only a short flight and hotel room away. We will shop, sightsee, and sample some of the fine cuisine New York offers. A carriage ride through Central Park will highlight what will be a fantastic weekend.

"Just the trip to New York is in itself fantastic! We'll leave town on _____"
     (Date)

_____
(My Signature)

Samuel Singleton

Because I Love You Gift Certificate

Dancing

We're young! Vibrant! Hip! Most of all, we're in love. We've kept up the latest must, dance step, and where it's happening.

We'll leave early and grab a light meal (we need to be light on our feet), and then head to the club. Drinks? Who needs it? Having you in my arms tonight is the only "high" I'll need. And just having you by my side in the morning will ensure my hangover will be one I can live with.

"Dancing? Party? Sign me up on _____"
                                    (Date)

_____
(My signature)

Samuel Singleton

Dancing

We're young! Vibrant! Hip! Most of all, we're in love. We've kept up the latest must, dance step, and where it's happening.

We'll leave early and grab a light meal (we need to be light on our feet), and then head to the club. Drinks? Who needs it? Having you in my arms tonight is the only "high" I'll need. And just having you by my side in the morning will ensure my hangover will be one I can live with.

"Dancing? Party? Sign me up on _____"
  (Date)

_____
(My signature)

Because I Love You Gift Certificate

Dancing

We're young! Vibrant! Hip! Most of all, we're in love. We've kept up the latest must, dance step, and where it's happening.

We'll leave early and grab a light meal (we need to be light on our feet), and then head to the club. Drinks? Who needs it? Having you in my arms tonight is the only "high" I'll need. And just having you by my side in the morning will ensure my hangover will be one I can live with.

"Dancing? Party? Sign me up on _____"
(Date)

_____
(My signature)

Samuel Singleton

Dancing

We're young! Vibrant! Hip! Most of all, we're in love. We've kept up the latest must, dance step, and where it's happening.

We'll leave early and grab a light meal (we need to be light on our feet), and then head to the club. Drinks? Who needs it? Having you in my arms tonight is the only "high" I'll need. And just having you by my side in the morning will ensure my hangover will be one I can live with.

"Dancing? Party? Sign me up on _____"
                                    (Date)

_____
(My signature)

Because I Love You Gift Certificate

Dancing

We're young! Vibrant! Hip! Most of all, we're in love. We've kept up the latest must, dance step, and where it's happening.

We'll leave early and grab a light meal (we need to be light on our feet), and then head to the club. Drinks? Who needs it? Having you in my arms tonight is the only "high" I'll need. And just having you by my side in the morning will ensure my hangover will be one I can live with.

"Dancing? Party? Sign me up on _____"
                                    (Date)

_____
(My signature)

Samuel Singleton

Dancing

We're young! Vibrant! Hip! Most of all, we're in love. We've kept up the latest must, dance step, and where it's happening.

We'll leave early and grab a light meal (we need to be light on our feet), and then head to the club. Drinks? Who needs it? Having you in my arms tonight is the only "high" I'll need. And just having you by my side in the morning will ensure my hangover will be one I can live with.

"Dancing? Party? Sign me up on _____"
                                    (Date)

_____
(My signature)

Because I Love You Gift Certificate

Dancing

We're young! Vibrant! Hip! Most of all, we're in love. We've kept up the latest must, dance step, and where it's happening.

We'll leave early and grab a light meal (we need to be light on our feet), and then head to the club. Drinks? Who needs it? Having you in my arms tonight is the only "high" I'll need. And just having you by my side in the morning will ensure my hangover will be one I can live with.

"Dancing? Party? Sign me up on _____"
(Date)

_____
(My signature)

Samuel Singleton

Because I Love You Gift Certificate

A Trip to Nowhere

Spontaneity, not variety, is the spice of life. Let me prove this to you. One weekend I'll drop by and say those fateful words. "Let's go!" Where? It really doesn't matter. All I want is for the two of us to be together.

I may bas up the car and we'll head west. If the traffic gets heavy we'll just rememer that there's no law which says we can't turn south. We'll visit historic homes, stop by roadside markets to shop, talk with interesting people who will tell us something we didn't know, and, if necessary, find a Bed and Breakfast to spend the night.

If our trip lasts longer than expected, we can always fall back on those immortal words on Monday morning. "I'm feeling real bad and I can't come in today."

"Ok! Just one thing though. Let's put the top down. Then we can leave on _____"
        (Date)

_____
(My signature)

Samuel Singleton

A Trip to Nowhere

Spontaneity, not variety, is the spice of life. Let me prove this to you. One weekend I'll drop by and say those fateful words. "Let's go!" Where? It really doesn't matter. All I want is for the two of us to be together.

I may bas up the car and we'll head west. If the traffic gets heavy we'll just rememer that there's no law which says we can't turn south. We'll visit historic homes, stop by roadside markets to shop, talk with interesting people who will tell us something we didn't know, and, if necessary, find a Bed and Breakfast to spend the night.

If our trip lasts longer than expected, we can always fall back on those immortal words on Monday morning. "I'm feeling real bad and I can't come in today."

"Ok! Just one thing though. Let's put the top down. Then we can leave on _____"
      (Date)

_____
(My signature)

Because I Love You Gift Certificate

A Trip to Nowhere

Spontaneity, not variety, is the spice of life. Let me prove this to you. One weekend I'll drop by and say those fateful words. "Let's go!" Where? It really doesn't matter. All I want is for the two of us to be together.

I may bas up the car and we'll head west. If the traffic gets heavy we'll just rememer that there's no law which says we can't turn south. We'll visit historic homes, stop by roadside markets to shop, talk with interesting people who will tell us something we didn't know, and, if necessary, find a Bed and Breakfast to spend the night.

If our trip lasts longer than expected, we can always fall back on those immortal words on Monday morning. "I'm feeling real bad and I can't come in today."

"Ok! Just one thing though. Let's put the top down. Then we can leave on _____"
      (Date)

_____
(My signature)

Samuel Singleton

A Trip to Nowhere

Spontaneity, not variety, is the spice of life. Let me prove this to you. One weekend I'll drop by and say those fateful words. "Let's go!" Where? It really doesn't matter. All I want is for the two of us to be together.

I may bas up the car and we'll head west. If the traffic gets heavy we'll just rememer that there's no law which says we can't turn south. We'll visit historic homes, stop by roadside markets to shop, talk with interesting people who will tell us something we didn't know, and, if necessary, find a Bed and Breakfast to spend the night.

If our trip lasts longer than expected, we can always fall back on those immortal words on Monday morning. "I'm feeling real bad and I can't come in today."

"Ok! Just one thing though. Let's put the top down. Then we can leave on _____"
      (Date)

      _____
      (My signature)

Because I Love You Gift Certificate

A Trip to Nowhere

Spontaneity, not variety, is the spice of life. Let me prove this to you. One weekend I'll drop by and say those fateful words. "Let's go!" Where? It really doesn't matter. All I want is for the two of us to be together.

I may bas up the car and we'll head west. If the traffic gets heavy we'll just rememer that there's no law which says we can't turn south. We'll visit historic homes, stop by roadside markets to shop, talk with interesting people who will tell us something we didn't know, and, if necessary, find a Bed and Breakfast to spend the night.

If our trip lasts longer than expected, we can always fall back on those immortal words on Monday morning. "I'm feeling real bad and I can't come in today."

"Ok! Just one thing though. Let's put the top down. Then we can leave on _____ "
          (Date)

_____
(My signature)

Samuel Singleton

A Trip to Nowhere

Spontaneity, not variety, is the spice of life. Let me prove this to you. One weekend I'll drop by and say those fateful words. "Let's go!" Where? It really doesn't matter. All I want is for the two of us to be together.

I may bas up the car and we'll head west. If the traffic gets heavy we'll just rememer that there's no law which says we can't turn south. We'll visit historic homes, stop by roadside markets to shop, talk with interesting people who will tell us something we didn't know, and, if necessary, find a Bed and Breakfast to spend the night.

If our trip lasts longer than expected, we can always fall back on those immortal words on Monday morning. "I'm feeling real bad and I can't come in today."

"Ok! Just one thing though. Let's put the top down. Then we can leave on _____"
        (Date)

_____
(My signature)

Because I Love You Gift Certificate

A Trip to Nowhere

Spontaneity, not variety, is the spice of life. Let me prove this to you. One weekend I'll drop by and say those fateful words. "Let's go!" Where? It really doesn't matter. All I want is for the two of us to be together.

I may bas up the car and we'll head west. If the traffic gets heavy we'll just rememer that there's no law which says we can't turn south. We'll visit historic homes, stop by roadside markets to shop, talk with interesting people who will tell us something we didn't know, and, if necessary, find a Bed and Breakfast to spend the night.

If our trip lasts longer than expected, we can always fall back on those immortal words on Monday morning. "I'm feeling real bad and I can't come in today."

"Ok! Just one thing though. Let's put the top down. Then we can leave on _____"
　　　　　(Date)

_____
(My signature)

Samuel Singleton

Because I Love You Gift Certificate

A Relaxing day at the Zoo

Most aren't like the one in San Diego, Ca., but there are Zoos around the United States that offer the same amount of knowledge and excitement. I've been able to locate Zoos that have Cheetahs, Lions, Bears, and that huge snake, the Anaconda! Since Elephants and Giraffes are still popular we'll drop by their homes. Hey! Let's just see everything!

"A day at the Zoo with you! I'm ready on "
(Date)

_____
(My Signature)

Samuel Singleton

A Relaxing day at the Zoo

Most aren't like the one in San Diego, Ca., but there are Zoos around the United States that offer the same amount of knowledge and excitement. I've been able to locate Zoos that have Cheetahs, Lions, Bears, and that huge snake, the Anaconda! Since Elephants and Giraffes are still popular we'll drop by their homes. Hey! Let's just see everything!

"A day at the Zoo with you! I'm ready on "
(Date)

_____
(My Signature)

Because I Love You Gift Certificate

A Relaxing day at the Zoo

Most aren't like the one in San Diego, Ca., but there are Zoos around the United States that offer the same amount of knowledge and excitement. I've been able to locate Zoos that have Cheetahs, Lions, Bears, and that huge snake, the Anaconda! Since Elephants and Giraffes are still popular we'll drop by their homes. Hey! Let's just see everything!

"A day at the Zoo with you! I'm ready on _____"
(Date)

_____
(My Signature)

Samuel Singleton

A Relaxing day at the Zoo

Most aren't like the one in San Diego, Ca., but there are Zoos around the United States that offer the same amount of knowledge and excitement. I've been able to locate Zoos that have Cheetahs, Lions, Bears, and that huge snake, the Anaconda! Since Elephants and Giraffes are still popular we'll drop by their homes. Hey! Let's just see everything!

"A day at the Zoo with you! I'm ready on _____"
                                                (Date)

_____
(My Signature)

Because I Love You Gift Certificate

A Relaxing day at the Zoo

Most aren't like the one in San Diego, Ca., but there are Zoos around the United States that offer the same amount of knowledge and excitement. I've been able to locate Zoos that have Cheetahs, Lions, Bears, and that huge snake, the Anaconda! Since Elephants and Giraffes are still popular we'll drop by their homes. Hey! Let's just see everything!

"A day at the Zoo with you! I'm ready on _____"
(Date)

_____
(My Signature)

Samuel Singleton

A Relaxing day at the Zoo

Most aren't like the one in San Diego, Ca., but there are Zoos around the United States that offer the same amount of knowledge and excitement. I've been able to locate Zoos that have Cheetahs, Lions, Bears, and that huge snake, the Anaconda! Since Elephants and Giraffes are still popular we'll drop by their homes. Hey! Let's just see everything!

"A day at the Zoo with you! I'm ready on _____"
                                                    (Date)

_____
(My Signature)

Because I Love You Gift Certificate

A Relaxing day at the Zoo

Most aren't like the one in San Diego, Ca., but there are Zoos around the United States that offer the same amount of knowledge and excitement. I've been able to locate Zoos that have Cheetahs, Lions, Bears, and that huge snake, the Anaconda! Since Elephants and Giraffes are still popular we'll drop by their homes. Hey! Let's just see everything!

"A day at the Zoo with you! I'm ready on "
(Date)

_____
(My Signature)

Samuel Singleton

Because I Love You Gift Certificate

Camping

It isn't for everyone, but I'm sure you and I can find a couple of friends to help us enjoy the great outdoors. We've talked about doing just this. Now is the time to put those words into action.

I have the tent, fishing gear, and I'll make sure I pack the insect repellent. We will see the squirrels at play, get a glimpse of the Eagles as they soar overhead, and witness firsthand, the absolute joy the world and nature has to offer us.

"The weather is just right. Let's leave on _____"
                                                (Date)

_____
(My Signature)

Camping

It isn't for everyone, but I'm sure you and I can find a couple of friends to help us enjoy the great outdoors. We've talked about doing just this. Now is the time to put those words into action.

I have the tent, fishing gear, and I'll make sure I pack the insect repellent. We will see the squirrels at play, get a glimpse of the Eagles as they soar overhead, and witness firsthand, the absolute joy the world and nature has to offer us.

"The weather is just right. Let's leave on _____"
                                                (Date)

_____
(My Signature)

Because I Love You Gift Certificate

Camping

It isn't for everyone, but I'm sure you and I can find a couple of friends to help us enjoy the great outdoors. We've talked about doing just this. Now is the time to put those words into action.

I have the tent, fishing gear, and I'll make sure I pack the insect repellent. We will see the squirrels at play, get a glimpse of the Eagles as they soar overhead, and witness firsthand, the absolute joy the world and nature has to offer us.

"The weather is just right. Let's leave on _____"
                                                          (Date)

_____
(My Signature)

Samuel Singleton

Camping

It isn't for everyone, but I'm sure you and I can find a couple of friends to help us enjoy the great outdoors. We've talked about doing just this. Now is the time to put those words into action.

I have the tent, fishing gear, and I'll make sure I pack the insect repellent. We will see the squirrels at play, get a glimpse of the Eagles as they soar overhead, and witness firsthand, the absolute joy the world and nature has to offer us.

"The weather is just right. Let's leave on _____"
                                                (Date)

_____
(My Signature)

Because I Love You Gift Certificate

Camping

It isn't for everyone, but I'm sure you and I can find a couple of friends to help us enjoy the great outdoors. We've talked about doing just this. Now is the time to put those words into action.

I have the tent, fishing gear, and I'll make sure I pack the insect repellent. We will see the squirrels at play, get a glimpse of the Eagles as they soar overhead, and witness firsthand, the absolute joy the world and nature has to offer us.

"The weather is just right. Let's leave on _____"
                                                                (Date)

_____
(My Signature)

Samuel Singleton

Camping

It isn't for everyone, but I'm sure you and I can find a couple of friends to help us enjoy the great outdoors. We've talked about doing just this. Now is the time to put those words into action.

I have the tent, fishing gear, and I'll make sure I pack the insect repellent. We will see the squirrels at play, get a glimpse of the Eagles as they soar overhead, and witness firsthand, the absolute joy the world and nature has to offer us.

"The weather is just right. Let's leave on _____"
(Date)

_____
(My Signature)

Because I Love You Gift Certificate

Camping

It isn't for everyone, but I'm sure you and I can find a couple of friends to help us enjoy the great outdoors. We've talked about doing just this. Now is the time to put those words into action.

I have the tent, fishing gear, and I'll make sure I pack the insect repellent. We will see the squirrels at play, get a glimpse of the Eagles as they soar overhead, and witness firsthand, the absolute joy the world and nature has to offer us.

"The weather is just right. Let's leave on _____"
(Date)

_____
(My Signature)

Samuel Singleton

Because I Love You Gift Certificate

Sailing

The ocean is a thing of beauty. It's water has the ability to look as though you are sailing over a deep blue glass. It seems as though the ocean will break should you reach down and touch it, even slightly.

We will choose a day so calm that it will seem as though this will indeed happen. A short trip from one port to another is all it'll take to make you feel calm and relaxed. A light meal on a hotel veranda overlooking that same blue ocean will make this a day we'll repeat over and over again.

"Maybe we can spot Moby Dick out there. I'm ready to shove off on _____."
(Date)

(My Signature)

Samuel Singleton

Sailing

The ocean is a thing of beauty. It's water has the ability to look as though you are sailing over a deep blue glass. It seems as though the ocean will break should you reach down and touch it, even slightly.

We will choose a day so calm that it will seem as though this will indeed happen. A short trip from one port to another is all it'll take to make you feel calm and relaxed. A light meal on a hotel veranda overlooking that same blue ocean will make this a day we'll repeat over and over again.

"Maybe we can spot Moby Dick out there. I'm ready to shove off on _____"
    (Date)

_____
(My Signature)

Because I Love You Gift Certificate

Sailing

The ocean is a thing of beauty. It's water has the ability to look as though you are sailing over a deep blue glass. It seems as though the ocean will break should you reach down and touch it, even slightly.

We will choose a day so calm that it will seem as though this will indeed happen. A short trip from one port to another is all it'll take to make you feel calm and relaxed. A light meal on a hotel veranda overlooking that same blue ocean will make this a day we'll repeat over and over again.

"Maybe we can spot Moby Dick out there. I'm ready to shove off on _____."
    (Date)

(My Signature)

Samuel Singleton

Sailing

    The ocean is a thing of beauty. It's water has the ability to look as though you are sailing over a deep blue glass. It seems as though the ocean will break should you reach down and touch it, even slightly.

    We will choose a day so calm that it will seem as though this will indeed happen. A short trip from one port to another is all it'll take to make you feel calm and relaxed. A light meal on a hotel veranda overlooking that same blue ocean will make this a day we'll repeat over and over again.

    "Maybe we can spot Moby Dick out there. I'm ready to shove off on _____."
    (Date)

_____
(My Signature)

Because I Love You Gift Certificate

Sailing

The ocean is a thing of beauty. It's water has the ability to look as though you are sailing over a deep blue glass. It seems as though the ocean will break should you reach down and touch it, even slightly.

We will choose a day so calm that it will seem as though this will indeed happen. A short trip from one port to another is all it'll take to make you feel calm and relaxed. A light meal on a hotel veranda overlooking that same blue ocean will make this a day we'll repeat over and over again.

"Maybe we can spot Moby Dick out there. I'm ready to shove off on _____"
    (Date)

(My Signature)

Samuel Singleton

Sailing

    The ocean is a thing of beauty. It's water has the ability to look as though you are sailing over a deep blue glass. It seems as though the ocean will break should you reach down and touch it, even slightly.

    We will choose a day so calm that it will seem as though this will indeed happen. A short trip from one port to another is all it'll take to make you feel calm and relaxed. A light meal on a hotel veranda overlooking that same blue ocean will make this a day we'll repeat over and over again.

    "Maybe we can spot Moby Dick out there. I'm ready to shove off on _____"
      (Date)

_____
(My Signature)

Because I Love You Gift Certificate

Sailing

The ocean is a thing of beauty. It's water has the ability to look as though you are sailing over a deep blue glass. It seems as though the ocean will break should you reach down and touch it, even slightly.

We will choose a day so calm that it will seem as though this will indeed happen. A short trip from one port to another is all it'll take to make you feel calm and relaxed. A light meal on a hotel veranda overlooking that same blue ocean will make this a day we'll repeat over and over again.

"Maybe we can spot Moby Dick out there. I'm ready to shove off on _____"
    (Date)

(My Signature)

Samuel Singleton

Because I Love You Gift Certificate

Go Kart Racing

Well, it isn't the Daytona Beach 500, but it'll seem like it as you and I race around that oval tract. Riding along the interstate can be fun but we always have to watch out for the police and other drivers.

Go Kart racing gives us the opportunity to throw all caution to the win. We'll zoom around the tract, feeling as free as a bird leaving its nest for the first time. We won't have to worry about red lights or a speed limit. Come with me. Let's have some fun!

"No police to worry about! _____ is the day I'll be ready to drive."　　　　　　　　　　　　　(Date)

_____
My Signature

Samuel Singleton

Go Kart Racing

Well, it isn't the Daytona Beach 500, but it'll seem like it as you and I race around that oval tract. Riding along the interstate can be fun but we always have to watch out for the police and other drivers.

Go Kart racing gives us the opportunity to throw all caution to the win. We'll zoom around the tract, feeling as free as a bird leaving its nest for the first time. We won't have to worry about red lights or a speed limit. Come with me. Let's have some fun!

"No police to worry about! _____ is the day I'll be ready to drive."
(Date)

_____
My Signature

Because I Love You Gift Certificate

Go Kart Racing

Well, it isn't the Daytona Beach 500, but it'll seem like it as you and I race around that oval tract. Riding along the interstate can be fun but we always have to watch out for the police and other drivers.

Go Kart racing gives us the opportunity to throw all caution to the win. We'll zoom around the tract, feeling as free as a bird leaving its nest for the first time. We won't have to worry about red lights or a speed limit. Come with me. Let's have some fun!

"No police to worry about! _____ is the day I'll be ready to drive."   (Date)

_____
My Signature

Samuel Singleton

Go Kart Racing

Well, it isn't the Daytona Beach 500, but it'll seem like it as you and I race around that oval tract. Riding along the interstate can be fun but we always have to watch out for the police and other drivers.

Go Kart racing gives us the opportunity to throw all caution to the win. We'll zoom around the tract, feeling as free as a bird leaving its nest for the first time. We won't have to worry about red lights or a speed limit. Come with me. Let's have some fun!

"No police to worry about! _____ is the day I'll be ready to drive."   (Date)

_____
My Signature

Because I Love You Gift Certificate

Go Kart Racing

Well, it isn't the Daytona Beach 500, but it'll seem like it as you and I race around that oval tract. Riding along the interstate can be fun but we always have to watch out for the police and other drivers.

Go Kart racing gives us the opportunity to throw all caution to the win. We'll zoom around the tract, feeling as free as a bird leaving its nest for the first time. We won't have to worry about red lights or a speed limit. Come with me. Let's have some fun!

"No police to worry about! _____ is the day I'll be ready to drive."   (Date)

_____
My Signature

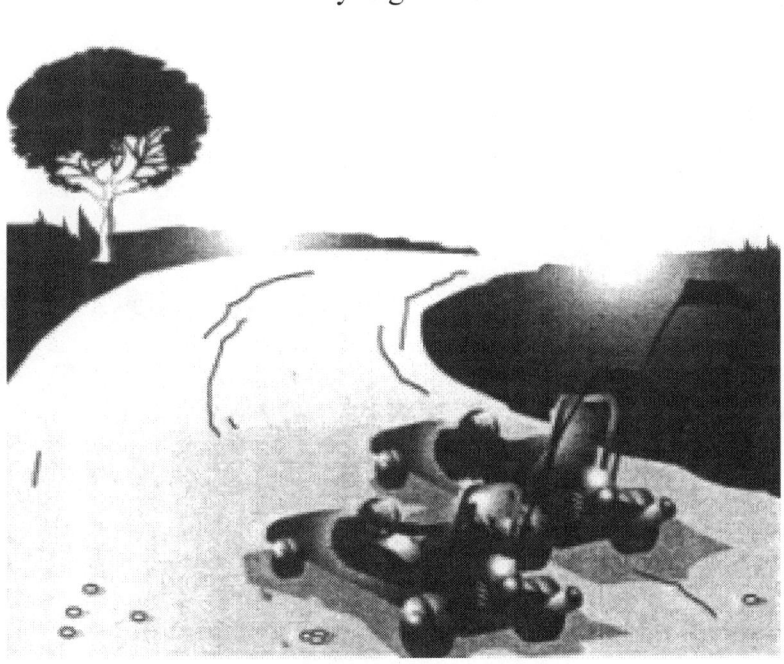

Samuel Singleton

Go Kart Racing

Well, it isn't the Daytona Beach 500, but it'll seem like it as you and I race around that oval tract. Riding along the interstate can be fun but we always have to watch out for the police and other drivers.

Go Kart racing gives us the opportunity to throw all caution to the win. We'll zoom around the tract, feeling as free as a bird leaving its nest for the first time. We won't have to worry about red lights or a speed limit. Come with me. Let's have some fun!

"No police to worry about! _____ is the day I'll be ready to drive."
(Date)

_____
My Signature

Because I Love You Gift Certificate

Go Kart Racing

Well, it isn't the Daytona Beach 500, but it'll seem like it as you and I race around that oval tract. Riding along the interstate can be fun but we always have to watch out for the police and other drivers.

Go Kart racing gives us the opportunity to throw all caution to the win. We'll zoom around the tract, feeling as free as a bird leaving its nest for the first time. We won't have to worry about red lights or a speed limit. Come with me. Let's have some fun!

"No police to worry about! _____ is the day I'll be ready to drive."
                                  (Date)

_____
My Signature

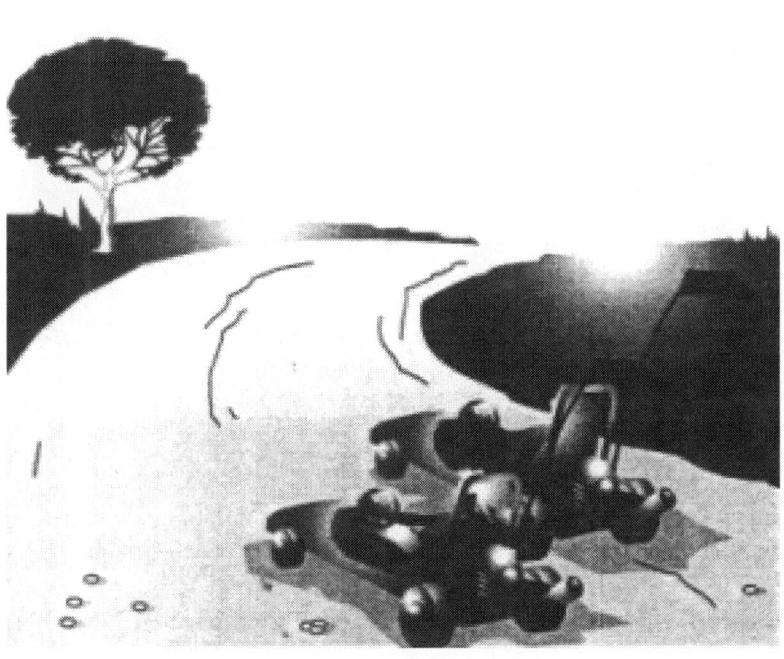

Samuel Singleton

Because I Love You Gift Certificate

Church

"Fate." "Luck." "The right place at the right time." These are but a few of the words and phrases used when describing how they met their mate. you and I know better.

We know that it was only through Gods divine guidance that you and I became one. We know that this was his plan long before we were born. So together you and I shall visit him each Sunday and revel in all his glory.

"The honor of escorting you to church is mine. I want us to do it every Sunday.

_____
(My Signature)

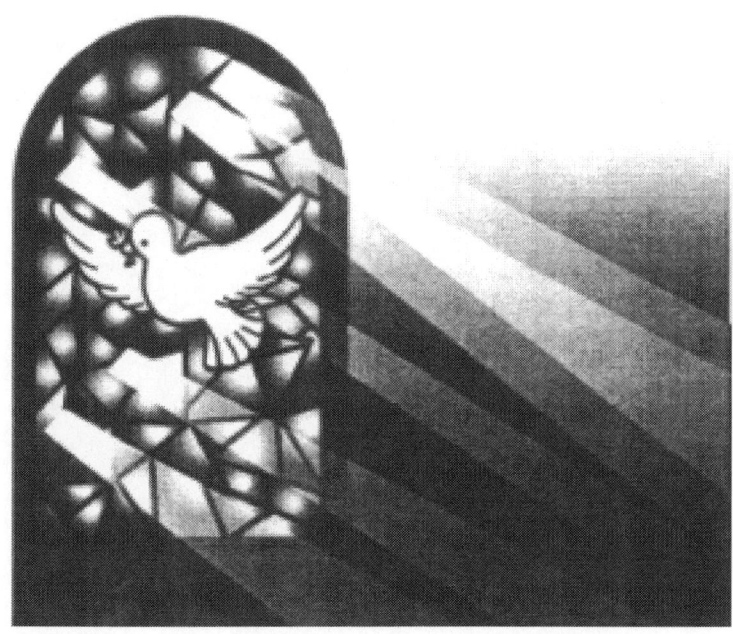

Samuel Singleton

Church

"Fate." "Luck." "The right place at the right time." These are but a few of the words and phrases used when describing how they met their mate. you and I know better.

We know that it was only through Gods divine guidance that you and I became one. We know that this was his plan long before we were born. So together you and I shall visit him each Sunday and revel in all his glory.

"The honor of escorting you to church is mine. I want us to do it every Sunday.

(My Signature)

Because I Love You Gift Certificate

Church

"Fate." "Luck." "The right place at the right time." These are but a few of the words and phrases used when describing how they met their mate. you and I know better.

We know that it was only through Gods divine guidance that you and I became one. We know that this was his plan long before we were born. So together you and I shall visit him each Sunday and revel in all his glory.

"The honor of escorting you to church is mine. I want us to do it every Sunday.

_____
(My Signature)

Church

"Fate." "Luck." "The right place at the right time." These are but a few of the words and phrases used when describing how they met their mate. you and I know better.

We know that it was only through Gods divine guidance that you and I became one. We know that this was his plan long before we were born. So together you and I shall visit him each Sunday and revel in all his glory.

"The honor of escorting you to church is mine. I want us to do it every Sunday.

_____
(My Signature)

Because I Love You Gift Certificate

Church

"Fate." "Luck." "The right place at the right time." These are but a few of the words and phrases used when describing how they met their mate. you and I know better.

We know that it was only through Gods divine guidance that you and I became one. We know that this was his plan long before we were born. So together you and I shall visit him each Sunday and revel in all his glory.

"The honor of escorting you to church is mine. I want us to do it every Sunday.

_____
(My Signature)

Samuel Singleton

Church

"Fate." "Luck." "The right place at the right time." These are but a few of the words and phrases used when describing how they met their mate. you and I know better.

We know that it was only through Gods divine guidance that you and I became one. We know that this was his plan long before we were born. So together you and I shall visit him each Sunday and revel in all his glory.

"The honor of escorting you to church is mine. I want us to do it every Sunday.

_____
(My Signature)

Because I Love You Gift Certificate

Church

"Fate." "Luck." "The right place at the right time." These are but a few of the words and phrases used when describing how they met their mate. you and I know better.

We know that it was only through Gods divine guidance that you and I became one. We know that this was his plan long before we were born. So together you and I shall visit him each Sunday and revel in all his glory.

"The honor of escorting you to church is mine. I want us to do it every Sunday.

_____
(My Signature)

Samuel Singleton

Because I Love You Gift Certificate

Jamaica

Even though it's only 500 miles southeast of the United States, once we set foot on Jamaica we'll feel as though we've entered another world.

Together, you and I will prove that there's more to the Island that beautiful beaches. We will walk hand in hand through Kingston as we visit Art Galleries and Museums, and we'll find out whey the British are crazy about Polo.

We will take that short trip to Montego Bay and visit Doctor's Cave Beach. Montego Bay is beautiful, and beauty deserves to meet beauty.

"Jamaica. Kingston. Montego Bay. All of this is doable to me on

----
(Date)

(My Signature)

Samuel Singleton

Jamaica

Even though it's only 500 miles southeast of the United States, once we set foot on Jamaica we'll feel as though we've entered another world.

Together, you and I will prove that there's more to the Island that beautiful beaches. We will walk hand in hand through Kingston as we visit Art Galleries and Museums, and we'll find out whey the British are crazy about Polo.

We will take that short trip to Montego Bay and visit Doctor's Cave Beach. Montego Bay is beautiful, and beauty deserves to meet beauty.

"Jamaica. Kingston. Montego Bay. All of this is doable to me on

_____
(Date)

_____
(My Signature)

Because I Love You Gift Certificate

Jamaica

Even though it's only 500 miles southeast of the United States, once we set foot on Jamaica we'll feel as though we've entered another world.

Together, you and I will prove that there's more to the Island that beautiful beaches. We will walk hand in hand through Kingston as we visit Art Galleries and Museums, and we'll find out whey the British are crazy about Polo.

We will take that short trip to Montego Bay and visit Doctor's Cave Beach. Montego Bay is beautiful, and beauty deserves to meet beauty.

"Jamaica. Kingston. Montego Bay. All of this is doable to me on

_____
(Date)

_____
(My Signature)

Samuel Singleton

Jamaica

Even though it's only 500 miles southeast of the United States, once we set foot on Jamaica we'll feel as though we've entered another world.

Together, you and I will prove that there's more to the Island that beautiful beaches. We will walk hand in hand through Kingston as we visit Art Galleries and Museums, and we'll find out whey the British are crazy about Polo.

We will take that short trip to Montego Bay and visit Doctor's Cave Beach. Montego Bay is beautiful, and beauty deserves to meet beauty.

"Jamaica. Kingston. Montego Bay. All of this is doable to me on

_____
(Date)

_____
(My Signature)

Because I Love You Gift Certificate

Jamaica

Even though it's only 500 miles southeast of the United States, once we set foot on Jamaica we'll feel as though we've entered another world.

Together, you and I will prove that there's more to the Island that beautiful beaches. We will walk hand in hand through Kingston as we visit Art Galleries and Museums, and we'll find out whey the British are crazy about Polo.

We will take that short trip to Montego Bay and visit Doctor's Cave Beach. Montego Bay is beautiful, and beauty deserves to meet beauty.

"Jamaica. Kingston. Montego Bay. All of this is doable to me on

_____
(Date)

_____
(My Signature)

Samuel Singleton

Jamaica

Even though it's only 500 miles southeast of the United States, once we set foot on Jamaica we'll feel as though we've entered another world.

Together, you and I will prove that there's more to the Island that beautiful beaches. We will walk hand in hand through Kingston as we visit Art Galleries and Museums, and we'll find out whey the British are crazy about Polo.

We will take that short trip to Montego Bay and visit Doctor's Cave Beach. Montego Bay is beautiful, and beauty deserves to meet beauty.

"Jamaica. Kingston. Montego Bay. All of this is doable to me on

_____
(Date)

_____
(My Signature)

Because I Love You Gift Certificate

Jamaica

Even though it's only 500 miles southeast of the United States, once we set foot on Jamaica we'll feel as though we've entered another world.

Together, you and I will prove that there's more to the Island that beautiful beaches. We will walk hand in hand through Kingston as we visit Art Galleries and Museums, and we'll find out whey the British are crazy about Polo.

We will take that short trip to Montego Bay and visit Doctor's Cave Beach. Montego Bay is beautiful, and beauty deserves to meet beauty.

"Jamaica. Kingston. Montego Bay. All of this is doable to me on

_____
(Date)

_____
(My Signature)

Samuel Singleton

A Stroll

Peole are in a hurry today. The Concord, the Internet, the Microwave, and Fast Food Restaurants all attest to the fact that man is constantly seeking instant gratification. "We want what we want and we want it now."

That's why I'm inviting you to take a stroll with me. A walk through the park as the squirrels gather nuts for winter, or just playing tag among themselves will be the best mental medicine we can get. We'll catch ants scurrying to and fro as they work to keep their colony thriving, and we'll marvel at the beauty of the Monarch Butterfly as it solftly alights on that one stranded rose.

The evening will end with us walking hand in hand, returning home just as dusk and darkness make their formal entrances.

"Walking in step with time is what I've always wanted to do. You and I can do this on _____."
  (Date)

_____
(My Signature)

Samuel Singleton

A Stroll

Peole are in a hurry today. The Concord, the Internet, the Microwave, and Fast Food Restaurants all attest to the fact that man is constantly seeking instant gratification. "We want what we want and we want it now."

That's why I'm inviting you to take a stroll with me. A walk through the park as the squirrels gather nuts for winter, or just playing tag among themselves will be the best mental medicine we can get. We'll catch ants scurrying to and fro as they work to keep their colony thriving, and we'll marvel at the beauty of the Monarch Butterfly as it solftly alights on that one stranded rose.

The evening will end with us walking hand in hand, returning home just as dusk and darkness make their formal entrances.

"Walking in step with time is what I've always wanted to do. You and I can do this on _____."
                    (Date)

_____
(My Signature)

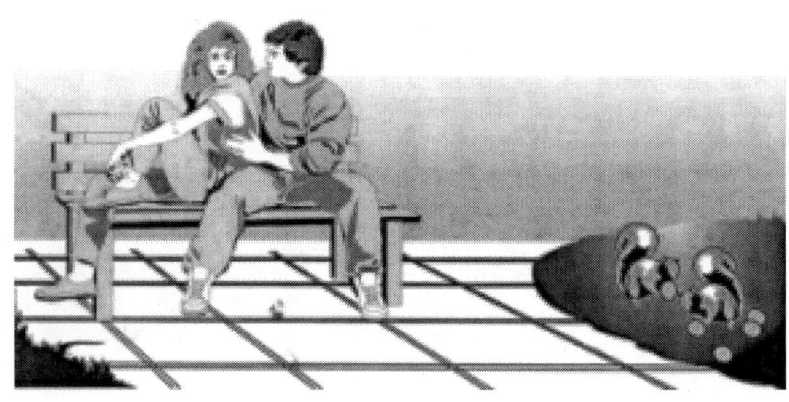

Because I Love You Gift Certificate

A Stroll

Peole are in a hurry today. The Concord, the Internet, the Microwave, and Fast Food Restaurants all attest to the fact that man is constantly seeking instant gratification. "We want what we want and we want it now."

That's why I'm inviting you to take a stroll with me. A walk through the park as the squirrels gather nuts for winter, or just playing tag among themselves will be the best mental medicine we can get. We'll catch ants scurrying to and fro as they work to keep their colony thriving, and we'll marvel at the beauty of the Monarch Butterfly as it solftly alights on that one stranded rose.

The evening will end with us walking hand in hand, returning home just as dusk and darkness make their formal entrances.

"Walking in step with time is what I've always wanted to do. You and I can do this on _____."
              (Date)

_____
(My Signature)

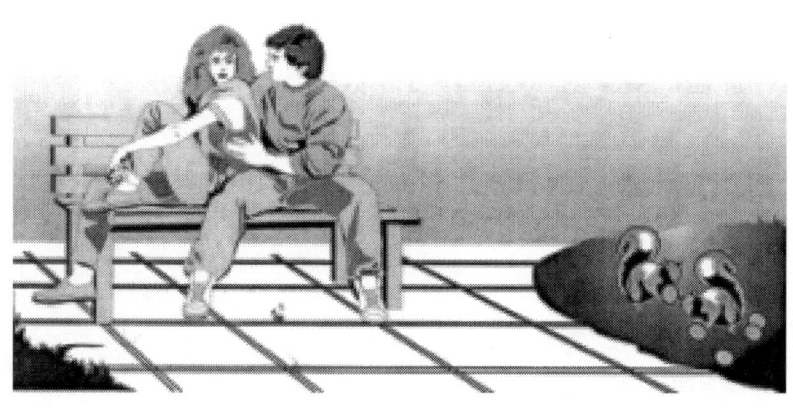

Samuel Singleton

A Stroll

Peole are in a hurry today. The Concord, the Internet, the Microwave, and Fast Food Restaurants all attest to the fact that man is constantly seeking instant gratification. "We want what we want and we want it now."

That's why I'm inviting you to take a stroll with me. A walk through the park as the squirrels gather nuts for winter, or just playing tag among themselves will be the best mental medicine we can get. We'll catch ants scurrying to and fro as they work to keep their colony thriving, and we'll marvel at the beauty of the Monarch Butterfly as it solftly alights on that one stranded rose.

The evening will end with us walking hand in hand, returning home just as dusk and darkness make their formal entrances.

"Walking in step with time is what I've always wanted to do. You and I can do this on _____."
 (Date)

_____
(My Signature)

Because I Love You Gift Certificate

A Stroll

Peole are in a hurry today. The Concord, the Internet, the Microwave, and Fast Food Restaurants all attest to the fact that man is constantly seeking instant gratification. "We want what we want and we want it now."

That's why I'm inviting you to take a stroll with me. A walk through the park as the squirrels gather nuts for winter, or just playing tag among themselves will be the best mental medicine we can get. We'll catch ants scurrying to and fro as they work to keep their colony thriving, and we'll marvel at the beauty of the Monarch Butterfly as it solftly alights on that one stranded rose.

The evening will end with us walking hand in hand, returning home just as dusk and darkness make their formal entrances.

"Walking in step with time is what I've always wanted to do. You and I can do this on _____."
(Date)

_____
(My Signature)

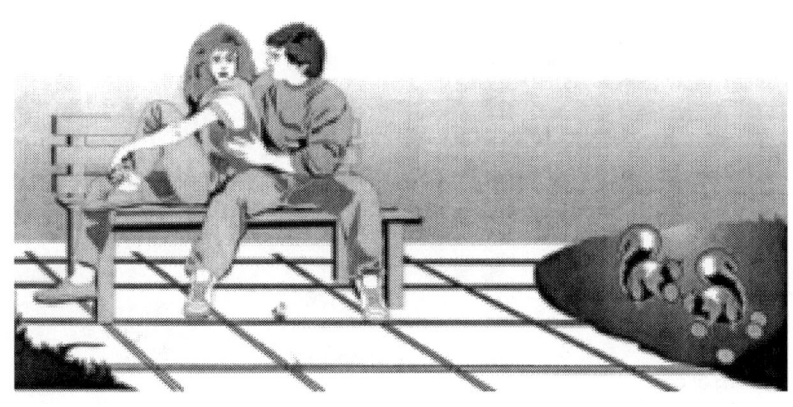

Samuel Singleton

A Stroll

Peole are in a hurry today. The Concord, the Internet, the Microwave, and Fast Food Restaurants all attest to the fact that man is constantly seeking instant gratification. "We want what we want and we want it now."

That's why I'm inviting you to take a stroll with me. A walk through the park as the squirrels gather nuts for winter, or just playing tag among themselves will be the best mental medicine we can get. We'll catch ants scurrying to and fro as they work to keep their colony thriving, and we'll marvel at the beauty of the Monarch Butterfly as it solftly alights on that one stranded rose.

The evening will end with us walking hand in hand, returning home just as dusk and darkness make their formal entrances.

"Walking in step with time is what I've always wanted to do. You and I can do this on _____."
(Date)

_____
(My Signature)

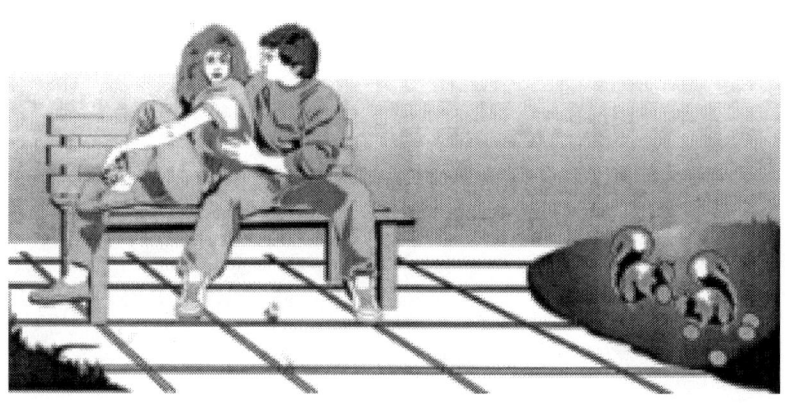

Because I Love You Gift Certificate

A Stroll

Peole are in a hurry today. The Concord, the Internet, the Microwave, and Fast Food Restaurants all attest to the fact that man is constantly seeking instant gratification. "We want what we want and we want it now."

That's why I'm inviting you to take a stroll with me. A walk through the park as the squirrels gather nuts for winter, or just playing tag among themselves will be the best mental medicine we can get. We'll catch ants scurrying to and fro as they work to keep their colony thriving, and we'll marvel at the beauty of the Monarch Butterfly as it solftly alights on that one stranded rose.

The evening will end with us walking hand in hand, returning home just as dusk and darkness make their formal entrances.

"Walking in step with time is what I've always wanted to do. You and I can do this on _____."
       (Date)

_____
(My Signature)

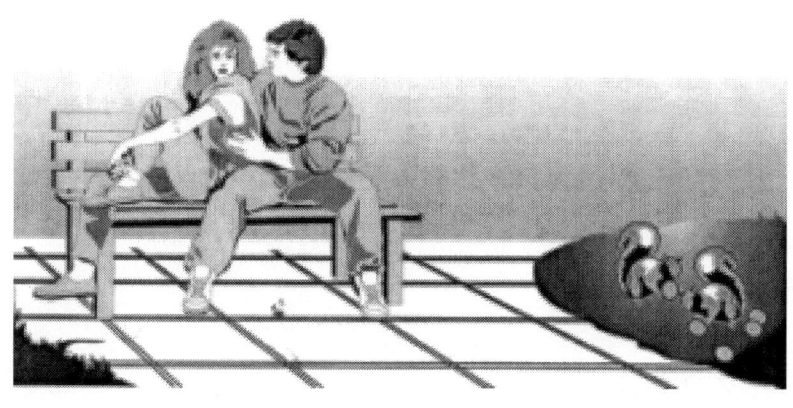

Samuel Singleton

Because I Love You Gift Certificate

Expensive Meal

That's what I want to give to you. The most expensive meal I can buy. How can I afford this, you ask? By spending my precious time preparing it.

I'll find the ingredients for your favorite desert. then I'll spend the afternoon preparing this wonderful meal just for you. What will be your job? Just keeping me company while I make a meal we shall not soon forget. Afterwards, I even do the dishes!

"I'm already hungry! We're eating on _____"
                                         (Date)

_____
(My Signature)

Samuel Singleton

Expensive Meal

That's what I want to give to you. The most expensive meal I can buy. How can I afford this, you ask? By spending my precious time preparing it.

I'll find the ingredients for your favorite desert. then I'll spend the afternoon preparing this wonderful meal just for you. What will be your job? Just keeping me company while I make a meal we shall not soon forget. Afterwards, I even do the dishes!

"I'm already hungry! We're eating on _____"
                                         (Date)

_____
(My Signature)

Because I Love You Gift Certificate

Expensive Meal

That's what I want to give to you. The most expensive meal I can buy. How can I afford this, you ask? By spending my precious time preparing it.

I'll find the ingredients for your favorite desert. then I'll spend the afternoon preparing this wonderful meal just for you. What will be your job? Just keeping me company while I make a meal we shall not soon forget. Afterwards, I even do the dishes!

"I'm already hungry! We're eating on _____"
                                         (Date)

_____
(My Signature)

Samuel Singleton

Expensive Meal

That's what I want to give to you. The most expensive meal I can buy. How can I afford this, you ask? By spending my precious time preparing it.

I'll find the ingredients for your favorite desert. then I'll spend the afternoon preparing this wonderful meal just for you. What will be your job? Just keeping me company while I make a meal we shall not soon forget. Afterwards, I even do the dishes!

"I'm already hungry! We're eating on _____"
                                                    (Date)

_____
(My Signature)

Because I Love You Gift Certificate

Expensive Meal

That's what I want to give to you. The most expensive meal I can buy. How can I afford this, you ask? By spending my precious time preparing it.

I'll find the ingredients for your favorite desert. then I'll spend the afternoon preparing this wonderful meal just for you. What will be your job? Just keeping me company while I make a meal we shall not soon forget. Afterwards, I even do the dishes!

"I'm already hungry! We're eating on _____"
(Date)

_____
(My Signature)

Samuel Singleton

Expensive Meal

That's what I want to give to you. The most expensive meal I can buy. How can I afford this, you ask? By spending my precious time preparing it.

I'll find the ingredients for your favorite desert. then I'll spend the afternoon preparing this wonderful meal just for you. What will be your job? Just keeping me company while I make a meal we shall not soon forget. Afterwards, I even do the dishes!

"I'm already hungry! We're eating on _____"
                                            (Date)

_____
(My Signature)

Because I Love You Gift Certificate

Expensive Meal

That's what I want to give to you. The most expensive meal I can buy. How can I afford this, you ask? By spending my precious time preparing it.

I'll find the ingredients for your favorite desert. Then I'll spend the afternoon preparing this wonderful meal just for you. What will be your job? Just keeping me company while I make a meal we shall not soon forget. Afterwards, I even do the dishes!

"I'm already hungry! We're eating on _____"
                                          (Date)

_____
(My Signature)

Made in the USA
Coppell, TX
22 December 2025

66952826R00081